LAURA OWEN & KORKY PAUL

Winnie AND Wilbur

WINNIE
Goes
Batty

OXFORD
UNIVERSITY PRESS

CONTENTS

WINNIE
Digs Deep

53

WINNIE
Goes Batty

75

Clowning
AROUND

'Coo, look at that!' said Winnie, giving
Wilbur a nudge. 'Ooo, look at that man
pretending to be a wheel! Look at that
lady standing on a horse! He hee, look
at the clowns! They look as silly as a
hippopotamus in pigtails!'

The circus had come to the village,
and everyone was there. Winnie had
never seen anything like it before.

'Look, look, Wilbur!' said Winnie,
flicking candyfloss in his face. 'Ha ha,

7

see that little dog stealing the sausages!'

Then suddenly, 'Ahhh!' The whole crowd sighed, and went quiet because they were seeing something beautiful.

'Oh!' said Winnie. 'Oo, just look at that! That's as blooming lovely as a butterfly ballet, that is!' Because a lady in a sparkly bathing costume was walking high up along a rope. The lady used an umbrella to help her balance. She threw sparkly sprinkles that winked and blinked as they fell down on to the crowd. 'Coo!' said Winnie. Everyone in the crowd clapped and cheered. Winnie looked around at their faces, wide open and smiling. The sparkly lady bowed, and everybody cheered.

'Hooray!' they shouted. 'Bravo!'
They whistled and they whooped
and they clapped.

'Ooo, Wilbur,' said Winnie. 'I'd love it
if people felt like that about me!'

As Winnie and Wilbur walked home,
Winnie tried walking along the lines in the
pavement, her arms out like an aeroplane.
Wibble-wobble, step-step.

'See?' said Winnie. 'I'm good at this!'

Then she tried walking along a garden
wall. **Wibble-wobble step-
whoops!** Winnie tried to balance herself
by waving one leg and two arms around.
'I'll do it along the washing line!' she told
Wilbur. 'Just like that lady!'

But by the time they got home Winnie
didn't just want to walk a tightrope.
She wanted to put on a whole circus
of her own.

'There's no point without people to see. I'll do it for the little ordinaries,' she said. 'They can cheer me and clap and say, "Ahh! Isn't she beeeeutiful!"'

'Mrrow!' said Wilbur, who didn't think that was very likely. But,

'Abracadabra!' went Winnie, and instantly poor Wilbur was in sparkly pants. 'You're my assistant,' said Winnie. 'Do a twirl!' **Twiddle-splat.** 'Try to be dignified,' said Winnie.

'Woof-he-hee!' laughed Scruff, looking through the fence from next door.

'You can be my other assistant!' said Winnie. '*Abracadabra!*'

And there was Scruff in a little sparkly waistcoat and a silly hat.

'Meeow-he-hee!'

Leap! Hiss! Pounce! Yap! They were soon chasing around the garden.

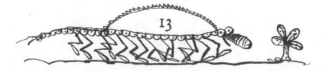

'Jerry!' called Winnie. 'Can you build me a tent, please?'

'If that's what you want, missus,' said Jerry, and he set to work.

Crash! Bang! Rip! Stitch! Heave-hup!

It wasn't long before a strange kind of big top had been made from a couple of trees, Winnie's curtains, and the tassels from her best underwear.

'Abracadabra!'

It had bunting and balloons and all sorts.

'Right!' said Winnie. 'Now we need to get the little ordinaries along to see my Show Of Beauty. I'll just ring Mrs Parmar.'

With the children on their way, Winnie made a few finishing touches to her big top. '*Abracadabra!*'

There was a sign for 'Winnie's Wanderful Circus Of Beautifulness!' '*Abracadabra!*'

There was a stall selling candy moss and snotty apples.

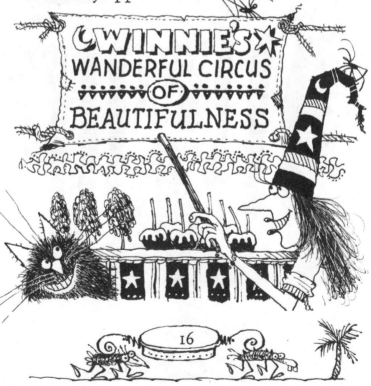

Then the little ordinaries came
marching up the path.

'Ooo!' they said when they saw the
big top.

'Urgh!' they said when they saw
the food.

Then the little ordinaries sat ready.

'Where's the show?' they said.

'Er ...' said Winnie. 'Er ... just
a moment. *Abracadabra!*'

17

And there was Winnie in the sparkliest
outfit a circus had ever seen. **Zing!**
glittered the sequins. **Twang!** went the
elastic where it was a bit too tight.

'When's it going to start?' shouted the
little ordinaries.

'I just need some music, please, Jerry,'
said Winnie.

'What?' said Jerry. 'You never said nuffink about music!'

'Boo!' went the little ordinaries.

'DO something!' said Winnie, at the bottom of the ladder. So,—

'**Um ti-ti, rum ti-ti,**' sang Jerry. While Scruff dug-dug-dug at a drum to make a drum-roll noise and **crash!** went Wilbur with a couple of saucepan lids.

19

'Here I go!' said Winnie. She climbed
up to the top of the ladder, then **wibble**
stepped one toe onto the washing line.
Wobble. Two feet . . . **Splat!** Winnie
fell head-first, onto her nose.

'Ha ha ha!' went the little ordinaries.

'Ouch!' said Winnie, sitting up and
rubbing her bright red nose.

'He hee hee!' went the little ordinaries.
'More! More!'

'Er . . . I'll do aerobatic broom riding,'
said Winnie. 'More music please, Jerry!'

'Tiddle-diddle-diddle . . . !'

Crash! Boom!

Winnie rose up on her broom. The little
ordinaries had seen her flying before.
Winnie went left. Winnie went right.

'Boring!' shouted the little ordinaries.

Winnie went up, then down.

'Boo!' shouted the little ordinaries.

'Watch this, then!' said Winnie. And **wibble-wobble-wibble** she carefully knelt on the broom as it flew. Then **wobble-wibble,** up onto one foot, and **wibble-wobble,** two feet. Up-up. Winnie stood up. Arms out, she rode the broomstick like a scarecrow on a surfboard.

'Ta-daa!' went Jerry.

'Ah!' gasped the crowd.

'Is it beeeutiful?' shouted Winnie.

'Meeeeooww!' went Wilbur.

But it was too late.

Splat! went Winnie into the side of
the tent, tangling like a fly in a spider's
web, upside-down and high above the
crowd.

'Help!' shouted Winnie.

'He hee! Ha haa!' laughed the little
ordinaries. 'Winnie's so funny!'

23

Jerry stepped forward and lifted Winnie down, although her sequinned slippers stayed up in the roof.

'You'll have to wear my shoes now, missus!' said Jerry, so Winnie put on Jerry's shoes. They were enormous.

'Ha ha!' went the little ordinaries. 'Winnie's a clown!'

24

'What?' said Winnie. But with her red
nose and the big shoes, she did look like
a clown. And as soon as she tried to walk
trip-bang! she fell over Scruff and
into a bucket of water.

'Stupid blooming dog!'
shouted Winnie.

'Ha ha haa!'

Winnie picked up another bucket of water and began to run after Scruff, and Wilbur chased after Winnie, and Jerry chased after Wilbur.

'Hooray!' shouted the crowd as Scruff and Winnie and Wilbur and Jerry fell **bump-bump-bump-bump!** into the sawdust.

Winnie sat up. She heard cheering and clapping and love.

'They blooming like us now that we're silly!' she said. 'Come on, Wilbur! Chase me up the ladder!' So off they went, chasing and falling and pushing and being daft.

'He hee, ho, ha!'

'Thank you, Winnie!' said Mrs Parmar.

26

'You were so funny, Winnie!' said the little ordinaries. 'We love you!'

'Really truly?' said Winnie. And she got out a huge spotty hankie and blew her nose on it. **Snort!** 'Who needs beauty when you can laugh, eh, Wilbur?'

27

WINNIE'S
Bubble Trouble

Glug-glug-slurp. 'Nice fizzy froggle-pop!' said Winnie. 'The trouble is that it blooming well bubbles up like frogspawn when I dance!' **Burp!**

Scrunch-munch-gulp. 'Meeew,' nodded Wilbur, scoffing crispy mouse tails as he waggled his hips and bopped along to the very loud Hobgoblins of Sound booming from Winnie's MP13 player.

It was a good party, even if it was just for the two of them. Even though there

was no reason for the party except that
they were bored. Still, Winnie and Wilbur
scoffed dandelion roots in slug-nettle dip.
Mouse rolls and turnip crisps. There were
balloons and streamer-weeds and party
splatters.

Bang! Wheeeee! Splat!

Winnie and Wilbur went to bed very
late. Wilbur went straight to sleep.

Snore, went Wilbur. **Snore-snore**
pause **snore** pause. **SNORE!**

'Oh, please shush, Wilbur!' said Winnie, lumping over in bed and putting her hands over her ears.

Snore-snore-snore pause **snore** paaaauuuussseee. **SNORE-splutter!**

31

'No!' wailed Winnie. 'I can't sleep with that noise!' She gave Wilbur a shove. Wilbur grunted and made silly noises with his lips. Then he went back to . . .

Snore-SNORE-snore pause.

Winnie put her pillow over her head,
but she was wide wide awake. And she
stayed wide awake for the rest of the
night.

'Ooo, my head hurts! That cat is
driving me as mad as a red-hot icicle!'

When the sun came up, Winnie got up
too, but she was bleary-eyed. She tried to
make breakfast.

Wail-wail-wail went the smoke
alarm as flames came from under the grill.

'Mrrow!' went Wilbur when she fed him his toadstool toasty.

'Have you not heard of "flame-grilling", you silly cat? That's posh cooking, that is!' But Wilbur spat the burnt toasty out and Winnie didn't fancy it either. So they opened a can of beans and ate those instead.

Then Winnie tried to tidy up all the
party mess.

Boom! The vacuum cleaner exploded.

Bang-splooosh! The washing
machine erupted.

'Mrr-he-he-hee!' laughed Wilbur.

Dust and rubbish and wet clothes and
soapy slippery water went everywhere.

And so did Winnie. **Slip-crash!** into
the dresser, so that saucepans and pots fell
to join the mess.

**Bang! Clang! Smash! Crash!
Ping!** Then, **brring-brrring!** the
telling-moan began to ring.

'Dimpled slug bottoms!' wailed Winnie, covering her ears. 'I wish I could float away from all this in a nice calm bubble, up into the clear quiet sky.' She reached for her wand. '*Abracadabra!*'

And instantly Winnie was in a serene soapy see-through bubble that glinted rainbow colours and floated, silently and smoothly, out through the window and up into the sky.

'Ah,' said Winnie. She closed her eyes and snoozed for a while as she just bubble-bobbed on the breeze, floating up and up. When she opened her eyes she saw birds and aeroplanes passing, but she couldn't hear them. 'Blissaramaroodles!' said Winnie.

39

Then she looked down. Her house was the size of a thumbnail. Wilbur looked the size of a flea.

'Oooer!' said Winnie, trying to stand up, but she couldn't stand up in the bubble. 'I'm too blooming high in the sky! Get me down! Where's my wand?' but if Winnie waved her wand she might pop the bubble. 'Oo dear, this must be what a dilly-duckling feels like squashed inside an egg!' said Winnie, feeling a bit panicky. 'I don't want to hatch in the sky! HELP!'

40

No sound came out of the bubble. But a small sound came within the bubble.

Parp!

'Whoops!' said Winnie.

The bubble swelled just a little bit.

'Pongy-wongy!' said Winnie. 'Why did I eat those blooming beans for breakfast? Wilbur, save me!'

Down on the ground, Wilbur put a paw to his brow and saw Winnie's bubble, tiny and far away.

'Meeeooww!' he called, and he looked around in panic. Winnie's broom would only fly for Winnie! He hadn't got a rocket! He hadn't got wings! He couldn't catapult himself! 'Oh, meeeow!' But Wilbur did have balloons left over from the party.

'Mroww!'

Wilbur grabbed balloon strings. He tied some to his tail and held tight to the others. Wilbur shoved **squeeeze-blop!** through the door. And he began to float up into the sky.

42

43

Up, up, until he was beside Winnie's
bubble. Winnie was waving and moving
her mouth.

'Get me out of this bubble of pongy
trouble bubble!' mouthed Winnie.

But how could Wilbur burst her bubble
without letting her fall from the sky?

'Mrrow!' Wilbur had an idea. He let go
of one balloon.

'Wilbur!' wailed Winnie, as Wilbur and
his balloons sank beneath her. But now
Wilbur's balloons were like a cushion
under Winnie's bubble. So Winnie could
pop her bubble and be safe. She poked
and poked with her wand and **pop!**
the bubble burst.

44

45

'Ah, fresh air!' said Winnie. 'Whoops!'
It isn't easy to balance on a pile of
balloons that are sinking quite fast under
your weight.

'Tweet tweet!'

'What the blooming . . . ?' began
Winnie as a flock of big-beaky
birdies flew alongside.

'A tweety-tweet treat!' went the birds,
thinking that Wilbur's purple balloons
looked like gigantic juicy grapes. So,—

Peck-pop! went one bird.

Peck-peck-pop-pop-pop! went

the others.

'Wiiiiillllbbbbuuuuurrr!' shouted
Winnie, as they sank faster and faster.
Winnie flapped her arms, trying to fly.
It didn't work, but it did remind Winnie
that she had her wand.

'Aaaabbrraaccaaddaabbrrraa!'
she shouted.

Next instant Winnie and Wilbur were
floating downwards slowly and gently,
holding on to a big parachute umbrella,
and . . . they landed in a lovely grassy
flowery meadow, soft and sweet smelling.

'Tweet-tweet!' sang some birdies.

'I don't want to hear any more from
you lot!' said Winnie.

She plucked furry caterpillars from a
leaf and put them into her ears as
earplugs. 'Oo, they tickle!' said Winnie.
'But I don't care. I've got peace AND I'm
safe on the ground!'

'Meeeow,' said Wilbur. *Yawn!
Yawn!* 'Me too!' said Winnie.

So they settled down in the grass and
sank into sleep. Until Wilbur began to
snore.

Snore-snore pause **grunt-sniffle.**

'Not again!' wailed Winnie. But it
wasn't very long before she was snoring
too.

SNORE! SNORE-SNORE! Grunt-
like-a-pig **SNOOOOORE!**

So it was only the birdies who had to
cover their ears.

WINNIE
Digs Deep

'Phewy-dewy, Wilbur, I'm as hot as a hot dog with ten hot-water bottles!' said Winnie. She emptied a jug of water over her head, and it steamed.

'Meow.' Wilbur was wilting too.

'This sunshine is going to melt us,' said Winnie. 'I'll soon be just a blooming pile of clothes on the pavement, and you'll just be a bit of black fluff and whiskers. Where can we find some shade?'

There was one place in the village that

53

was always cool, and that was the museum.
It had high ceilings and stone walls and it
echoed.

'Ahhh!' sighed Winnie.

Ahhhh! sighed the walls.

'Shushshsh!' said the attendant.

Shushshsh! said the walls.

So Winnie and Wilbur wandered around
the museum, looking at dinosaur bones.

'Scruff from next door would like to
chew on that one!' said Winnie.

'Shush!' said the attendant.

Shush! said the walls.

Winnie and Wilbur looked at glass cases full of dead insects and stuffed animals.

'That ugly one looks just like you!' said Winnie to Wilbur. 'Oh, it is you!' Because the glass case worked like a mirror. 'He hee, ha haa!'

He hee, ha haa went the walls.

'Shushsh!'

Shushsh!

56

'What else is there?' said Winnie.

There were cabinets full of cracked pots and bits of rusty metal pins and brooches and dirty bent old coins. Winnie wrinkled her nose.

'They're not very pretty! Why are they there?'

'Because,' said the attendant, wagging a finger, 'they is treasure and they is worth a very great deal of money! Now please shush, Modom, and please take that h'animal out of here. Such h'animals is not allowed in museums h'except when they is in a glass case, clearly labelled.'

'That's a silly rule!' said Winnie.

But she and Wilbur went back out into the sunshine.

'Meeeow?' asked Wilbur.

'We're going home to dig up our own treasure!' said Winnie. 'We can make a museum of our own!'

Winnie looked at her garden.

'Er ... where shall we begin digging? Oo, I know!' Winnie waved her wand. 'Abracadabra!'

Instantly Winnie had a metal detector in
her hand.

Buzz it went. **Buzz-buzz squeal!**

'Oo!' said Winnie. 'It's found
something already! Dig just there,
Wilbur!'

So Wilbur dug.

'Mrrow!' he said crossly. Digging is hot work when you are wearing a fur coat.

But, **dig-throw dig-throw** went Wilbur.

'Just a blooming button!' complained Winnie.

Squeeeaaal! insisted the metal detector.

'Keep digging!' said Winnie.

And suddenly Wilbur's paw hit something.

'Ooo, what is it?' asked Winnie, jumping up and down. 'Let me see! Oh! A rusty old baked has-beans can. Knitted blooming noodles, Wilbur! Let's try again.'

Buzz-buzz-buzz-squeal!

'What we need is someone who's really good at digging. Go and fetch Scruff!'

Wilbur dug. Winnie dug. Scruff came over from next door and he dug-dug-dug. Then Jerry came over with his giant spade and he DUG.

'Wow!' said Winnie as earth flew everywhere, and so did 'treasures'. There were old nails, a hair grip, a bent fork and some dentures.

'There must be some real treasure somewhere,' said Winnie. 'Dig a bit deeper, please, Jerry.'

'OK, missus,' said Jerry, and he dug
and dug, digging up cables and pipes and
bones.

'Ruff!' went Scruff.

'This is hot work!' said Jerry, so
Winnie brought out a big jug of seaweed
squash for them all. 'Er . . . I fink I'll give
that a miss, missus,' said Jerry, and he
went on digging.

DIG–DIG. As he dug, Jerry sank lower and lower until all that you could see was his curly hair level with the grass. A mountain of soil and bricks and roots was growing beside the hole.

'Have you found anything good yet?' asked Winnie.

'What about this fing?' Jerry handed up something round and metal and . . .

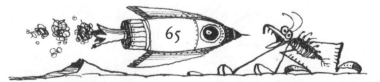

'Ooo!' said Winnie. 'It's a Viking helmet! Lost by a brave Viking who . . . Oh. Er . . . I think maybe it's just my old saucepan with the handle that came off. Try again, Jerry!'

Bleep-beeep-squeal! 'Try just down there!'

As the afternoon wore on, the hole got bigger, the soil mountain got bigger, and Winnie and Jerry and Wilbur and Scruff got hotter and tireder and crosser. The pile of found things got higher, but none of them looked to Winnie as though they would be worth 'the great deal of money' that the museum treasures were.

'You might like these!' said Jerry, and he held up something small and wriggly with lots of legs and eyes and tails and ears.

'Coo!' said Winnie. 'That's a brand new kind of bug! It looks yummy! Are there more of them, Jerry?'

'There's all sorts,' said Jerry.

So Winnie went down on a rope to
the bottom of the hole and she filled up
a bucket with deep-soil bugs.

It was trickier getting back up with
a bucketful of bugs.

'All yummy scrummy in my tummy!'
said Winnie. 'Oo, I wonder if the museum
would like to label some of them and put
them in a cabinet? I'll give that man a
moan call and see if he's interested.'

'Does you want me to go on
digging?' asked Jerry.

'Just one more dig for luck, please,
Jerry,' said Winnie. 'Then I'll get you a
bowl of pickle ice cream.' So . . .

Dig went Jerry, and suddenly,—

69

Whooosh! . . . water came gushing
into the hole. Up floated Jerry.

'Ah! That's nice!'

'Ruff-ruff!' barked Scruff, all excited.
He leapt into the water and
doggy-paddled round in circles.

'We've got our own blooming
swimming pool!' said Winnie. 'Come on,
Wilbur! Dive in!'

'Abracadabra!' went Winnie, and
instantly there was a slide down the
mountain of diggings, **wheee-splosh!**,
into the pool. **Wheee-splosh-yap!**
went Scruff. **Wheee-splash!** went
Wilbur. **Wheeee-Splooooosh!**
went Jerry, and the water rose higher.

Along came the museum attendant.
He looked at the pile of findings. He
rubbed his chin. He frowned. Then he
said, 'Modom, is you thinking of selling
those h'objects?'

'H'objects?' said Winnie. 'Oh, that
lot! You can have that load of junk for
nothing. I'll donate it. D'you want a
swim while you're here?'

'No, h'I think not, Modom,' said the
attendant, wiping sweat from under
his cap.

'Suit yourself,' said Winnie. 'Just put Jerry's and Scruff's and Wilbur's and my name on the label if you put anything in the display, will you? After all, we are the treasure seekers what found it.'

Then the four treasure seekers went mad in the treasure hole swimming pool, nibbling deep-soil bugs and ice-cream.

'Good friends are better blooming treasure than rusty old pins, if you ask me!' said Winnie.

WINNIE
Goes Batty

'Mmn. Yummy in my hungry tummy!'
said Winnie, licking her fingers. She was
sitting on the doorstep and munching
microwaved turnip chips dipped in snail
sauce. To microwave a frozen chip all you
had to do was wave your wand everso slightly
at it and **zap!** the chips were cooked. It was
very quick. 'Scrummy! Mmph!' said Winnie,
stuffing lots of chips into her mouth.

Then bossy sister Wilma came round
the corner.

'You do eat rubbish, Winnie!' said
Wilma, looking down her long nose.
'You're always eating fast food instead of
good, well-cooked home-made meals.
I don't think you look after yourself
properly, Winnie.'

'How can you call snail sauce fast?'
asked Winnie. 'Anyway, I do cook lovely
fresh food for Wilbur and for me. If you
saw what I'm cooking for tea tonight,
then you'd know.'

'All right, I'll come to tea and see for myself,' said Wilma.

'Oh, heck in a hat!' said Winnie. 'Bother. Er ... That'll be lovely. See you later, then, Wilma. Bye!'

Winnie hurried into the house.

'Wilbur?' she called. 'Where are you, Wilbur? You can come out now. She's gone, but she's coming back for tea, so we've got to cook up a feast. What shall we give her?' Winnie looked through her recipes. 'Hmm. I think we'll have pickled antchovies. Have we got any pickled ants, Wilbur?'

'Meeow,' said Wilbur, pointing at a jar.

'Good. Then we'll have squid in jelly.
Is there squid in the fridge?'

Wilbur opened the fridge door and
rummaged. 'Meeow.'

'Good. Then for the main course we'll
have my special batburger in a buttered
bun with roasted radish relish. Look in

the battery, please, Wilbur. Check how many bats we've got. We might have battenberg cake for afters, so we'll need plenty of bats.'

Wilbur opened the battery door.

'Mrrow!' said Wilbur.

'Knotted noodles, you're blooming right!' said Winnie, peering in. 'There's only one diddly little bat in there!'

The diddly little bat cowered in a corner. Its diddly little batty knees knocked together. It looked at Winnie with its diddly batty eyes.

'Mrrrow?' asked Wilbur, ready to pounce.

Squeak! went the diddly little bat.

81

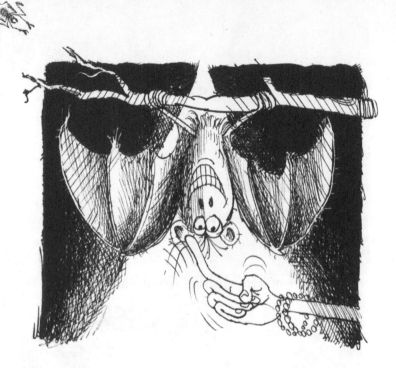

'Er ...' said Winnie. 'No, I don't think so, Wilbur.' She reached out a finger to stroke the soft diddly little batty velvety head. 'This one's too scraggy-scrawny to serve up to Wilma. Anyway, we need a whole bagful of bats. We'd best go to the Bat Caves and get some plump fresh ones to mash into burgers.'

So Winnie got shopping bags, and she
and Wilbur climbed onto the broom, and
off they flew. But Winnie was wriggling.
Jiggle-wiggle went the broom.
Swerve! went the broom.

'Meeow!' protested Wilbur.

'Sorry, Wilbur,' said Winnie.

'But there's something itching and scratching down my blooming front!' Winnie dipped her hand down the front of her dress. 'Heck and a half!' **Wobble!** 'What the flipping fly-swat is this?'

Winnie pulled out something small and black and trembling. 'It's that blooming diddly bat!' The diddly bat trembled in her fingers. 'Ah,' said Winnie, suddenly going soppy. 'Poor little thing!'

'Meeow!' went Wilbur.

'It just wants to go home to the Bat Cave,' said Winnie. 'Ah, bless its diddly little heart!' And she let the bat cling to her front like a brooch.

'Hmph!' said Wilbur.

85

'Here we are!' said Winnie.

They parked the broom outside the Bat Cave, and picked up batting nets.

'**Abracadabra!**' went Winnie.

Her wand began to glow brightly, lighting the cave, making shadows and showing bats clinging to all the walls.

Squeak! Squeak! Squeak! went the mass of bats.

'Pongy-wongy-woo!' said Winnie, holding her nose. 'These bats smell good and lively!'

Wilbur licked his lips. **Swat!** he went with his net.

Swish-swat! went Winnie.

'Got one!' she said.

But the diddly bat scrambled up Winnie's shoulder and squeaked in her ear.

Squeak!

'Oh!' said Winnie. 'That one's the diddly bat's mummy and he doesn't want her cooked into a burger.' So Winnie let that one go.

Swish-swish-swat! she caught another.

'I've got a good fat one here, Wilbur! It's as fat as a flump dumpling! Hold the wand-light so I can see it properly!' Then, 'Oh!' said Winnie, because the big fat bat was rubbing its eyes. 'This fat one's blooming well crying!' said Winnie.

Squeak! went the diddly bat.

'Fossilized fishcakes!' said Winnie. 'This fat one's your grandpa? Are you related to every bat in the whole blooming cave?'

88

Squeak!

Winnie put down her net. 'Oh, I give up! Come on, Wilbur. We'll have to cook something else. I'm not blooming-well eating something that's related to any friends of mine. I shall make Wilma a nice pondweed salad or something, and that'll have to do her. Come on!'

They flew back home, where they looked in the store cupboard.

90

'Aha! Bottled flies,' said Winnie.
'They'll have to do. And there's a packet
of sun dried lice too. Get out the pans,
Wilbur, she'll be here in five shakes of a
cockroach's bottom.'

Brrriiiinnnnggg!
Wiiiiinnnnniiiieeee! went the
dooryell.

'She's blooming here already! And I
haven't cooked a thing!' said Winnie.

Winnie opened the door, and there stood Wilma with her nose in the air, sniffing.

'What can you smell?' asked Winnie, a bit worried.

'Not a thing!' said Wilma. 'You've not done any cooking at all, have you, Winnie? I knew you wouldn't!'

'I was going to . . .'

'Huh!' said snooty Wilma. 'Going to isn't the same as doing. Are we to starve?'

But just then, a **sizzle** sound came from the kitchen, and a wonderful smell curled around the corner and up Wilma's nose.

'Oh!' she said, and she stepped into the kitchen. 'Your scraggy old cat is doing the cooking, Winnie! Oh, and he's being helped by . . . is that a bat?'

'It is,' said Winnie. 'That's my little diddly bat. And those are all his family!' she said, pointing around the room where bats were all being Wilbur's little helpers, stirring and chopping and fetching. One bat settled like a great velvet bow in Winnie's hair.

'I see!' said Wilma. 'So what are we going to eat? It does smell rather good!'

Winnie peered into the pans. 'Er . . . it's fly fritters with lice sprinkles.'

'Very nice,' said Wilma.

And it was.

And when Wilma had gone, Winnie looked around her batty room with the bats all hanging up to sleep.

'Night-night. Mind the cats don't bite,' said Winnie. She kissed the little diddly bat on the nose. 'D'you know, I think I'll join you!'

Winnie hung herself from the curtain pole
so that she could sleep like a bat, too. And
so did Wilbur, at least for a few seconds.

'Mrrow!'

Flump!

Enjoy more magic moments with **Winnie** AND **Wilbur**